AARON COPLAND

Old American Songs

Complete

© 1997 Al Hirschfeld. Art Reproduced by Special Arrangement with Hirschfeld's Exclusive Representative, The Margo Feiden Galleries Ltd., New York.

BOOSEY & HAWKES

AN IMAGEM COMPANY

DISTRIBUTED BY

HAL•LEONARD®
CORPORATION
7777 W. BLUEMOUND RD. P.O. BOX 13819 MILWAUKEE, WI 53213

www.boosey.com
www.halleonard.com

The first set of *Old American Songs* was completed in 1950, the same year that Copland finished his other major song set, *Twelve Poems of Emily Dickinson*. While Copland was writing the songs, tenor Peter Pears and composer Benjamin Britten came to visit him. Taken by Copland's new settings, they left with his promise of receiving copies of the songs in England to perform. On October 17, 1950, the first set was given its world premiere by Pears with Britten at the piano at their Aldeburgh Festival. The American premiere took place in New York on January 28, 1951, with Copland accompanying baritone William Warfield. The success of the first set prompted Copland to set five more songs. Finished in 1952, the second set was premiered by Warfield and Copland at the Castle Hill Concerts in Massachusetts on July 24 of that year. Copland would later orchestrate both sets for medium voice and small orchestra. Warfield sang the premiere of the orchestrated first set with the Los Angeles Philharmonic, conducted by Alfred Wallenstein, on January 7, 1955. Grace Bumbry premiered the second set with the Ojai Festival Orchestra on May 25, 1955, with Copland on the podium.

Contents

FIRST SET

1. *The Boatmen's Dance*
Published in Boston in 1843 as an "original banjo melody" by Old Dan. D. Emmett, who later composed Dixie. From the Harris Collection of American Poetry and Plays in Brown University.

2. *The Dodger*
As sung by Mrs. Emma Dusenberry of Mena, Arkansas, who learned it in the 1880's. Supposedly used in the Cleveland-Blaine presidential campaign. Published by John A. and Alan Lomax in *Our Singing Country*.

3. *Long Time Ago*
Issued in 1837 by George Pope Morris, who adapted the words, and Charles Edward Horn, who arranged the music from an anonymous, original minstrel tune. Also from the Harris Collection.

4. *Simple Gifts*
A favorite song of the Shaker sect, from the period 1837-1847. The melody and words were quoted by Edward D. Andrews in his book of Shaker rituals, songs and dances, entitled *The Gift To Be Simple*.

5. *I Bought Me a Cat*
A children's nonsense song. This version was sung to the composer by the American playwright Lynn Riggs, who learned it during his boyhood in Oklahoma.

SECOND SET

1. *The Little Horses*
A children's lullaby song originating in the Southern States – date unknown. This adaptation founded in part on John A. and Alan Lomax's version in *Folk Song U.S.A.*

2. *Zion's Walls*
A revivalist song. Original melody and words credited to John G. McCurry, compiler of the *Social Harp*. Published by George P. Jackson in *Down East Spirituals*.

3. *The Golden Willow Tree*
Variant of the well-known Anglo-American ballad, more usually called *The Golden Vanity*. This version is based on a recording issued by the Library of Congress Music Division from its collection of the Archive of American Folk Song. Justus Begley recorded it with banjo accompaniment for Alan and Elizabeth Lomax in 1937.

4. *At the River*
Hymn Tune. Words and melody are by Rev. Robert Lowry, 1865.

5. *Ching-a-ring Chaw*
Minstrel Song. The words have been adapted from the original, in the Harris Collection of American Poetry and Plays in Brown University.

Old American Songs

FIRST SET

1. THE BOATMEN'S DANCE
(Minstrel Song-1843)

Arranged by
AARON COPLAND

dance the boat-men dance O dance all night 'til broad day - light and go

home with the gals in the morn - in'.

As at first (♪ = 63)

ff *legato*

High row the boat-men row

float - in' down the riv - er, the O - hi - o,____ High row the

boat - men row float - in' down the riv - er, the O - hi - o.____

2. THE DODGER
(Campaign Song)

Arranged by
AARON COPLAND

look out girls — he's a - tell - in' you a lie Yes we're all

dodg - in', — a - dodg - in', dodg - in', dodg - in' Yes we're

all dodg - in' out a way through the

world. —

a tempo **mp**

(mark the bass)

ff

ff

sf *sf* *sf* *sf* *sf*

sf *sf*

3. LONG TIME AGO
(Ballad)

Arranged by
AARON COPLAND

Dwelt a maid be - loved and cher-ish'd By high and — low But the au - tumn leaf she per-ish'd Long time a - go. Rock and tree and flow - ing wa - ter Long time a - go

Bird and bee and blos - som taught her Love's __ spell __ to know __

While to my fond words she lis-ten'd Mur - mur - ing __

low Ten - der - ly her blue eyes glis-ten'd

Long time _ a - go. __

4. SIMPLE GIFTS

(Shaker Song)

Arranged by
AARON COPLAND

[2nd time to Coda]

love and de - light. _____ When true sim - pli - ci - ty is gained To

bow and to bend we shan't be a-shamed To turn, turn will be our de-light 'Till by

turn- ing, turn-ing we come round right. _____ 'Tis the

CODA

(dreamily)

5. I BOUGHT ME A CAT
(Children's Song)

Arranged by
AARON COPLAND

Old American Songs

SECOND SET

HIRSCHFELD 60

1. THE LITTLE HORSES
(Lullaby)

Arranged by
AARON COPLAND

Slowly, somewhat dragging (♪ = 76)

Hush you bye, Don't you cry, Go to sleep-y lit-tle ba - by. When you wake, You shall have, All the pret-ty lit-tle hor - ses.

Faster and rhythmically precise (*starting a little slowly*) Tempo II (♩ = 76)

Blacks and bays, Dap-ples and grays, Coach and six - a lit-tle hor - ses. Blacks and bays, Dap-ples and grays, Coach _____ and six - a lit-tle hor - ses. _

hold back

2. ZION'S WALLS

(Revivalist Song)

Arranged by
AARON COPLAND

3. THE GOLDEN WILLOW TREE

(Anglo-American Ballad)

Arranged by
AARON COPLAND

Gold-en Wil-low Tree, As she sailed in the low - land lone - some

low, As she sailed in the low - land so low.

We had-n't been a-sail-in' more than two weeks or three, Till we

came in sight of the Brit-ish Ro-ver-ie, As she sailed in the low -

I'll give thee, _____ the _ fair - est of my daugh-ters as she sails up - on the sea, If you'll sink 'em in the low - land lone - some low, If you'll sink 'em in the land that lies so low." _____ He

turned up-on his back and a - way swum he, He__ swum till he came to the

(r.h. glassy)
p

Brit-ish Ro - ver - ie, He had a lit - tle in - stru - ment fit - ted for his use, He__

bored nine holes and he bored them all at once. He turned up-on his breast and

back swum he, He__ swum till he came to the Gold-en Wil-low Tree.

"Cap-tain, O cap-tain, come take me on board,_____ O

Cap-tain, O Cap-tain, come take me on board,_____ And do un-to me as

good as your word For I sank 'em in the low - land lone-some

low, I sank 'em in the low - land so low."_____

"Oh no, I won't take you on board, Oh no, I won't take you on board, Nor do un-to you as good as my word, Though you sank 'em in the low - land lone - some

low, Though you sank 'em in the land that lies so

low." _____

f *(as at first)*

(p)

p

"If it was-n't for the love that I have for your men, I'd

do un-to you as I done un-to them, I'd sink you in the low -

(mp)

(poco accentuàto)

4. AT THE RIVER
(Hymn Tune)

Arranged by
AARON COPLAND

river, Gather with the saints by the river That

flows by the throne of God. *cresc.*

ff

Soon we'll reach the shin - ing

(cresc.)

ff

meno f

river, Soon our pil - grim-age will cease,

meno f

Soon our hap-py hearts will quiv - er With the mel - o - dy of peace.

Yes we'll gath - er by the riv - er, The beau - ti - ful, the beau - ti - ful river, Gath - er with the saints by the riv - er That flows by the throne of God, That flows by the throne of God.

5. CHING-A-RING CHAW
(Minstrel Song)

Arranged by
AARON COPLAND

style, Coach with four white hor - ses, There the eve - nin'

meal, Has one two three four cour - ses.

Ching-a-ring-a ring ching, ching - a ring ching, Ho - a ding-a ding kum lar - kee,

Ching-a-ring-a ring ching, Ho - a ding kum lar - kee.

Nights we all will dance, To the harp and